Magickal C

Attract Money Fast wit.
and Modern Wealth Magick

Damon Brand

THE GALLERY OF
MAGICK

CONTENTS

What Can This Book Do for You?

Magick can make you a lot wealthier than you are now. How wealthy you become is your choice.

You can attract a small amount of money, just once, and leave magick behind forever. Or you can keep using magick, adapting your life to build wealth.

Whether you want to get emergency cash or build a strong financial future, the Magical Cashbook is a powerful method for generating reasonable amounts of money, on an ongoing basis.

This small, simple book is easy to make. Essentially, you buy a notebook, cover it in symbols and perform a basic ritual to give it power. Despite the simple method, you can attract cash in a short length of time. The book takes a few minutes to make and charge, but then it works wonders.

It's well known that many famous occultists of old died in poverty. So why have I written a book on attracting money with magick?

We now have more knowledge and experience, and when certain conditions are met, magick works, and it works well. Satisfying these conditions is easy. I need to show you that money magick can work, and it can work easily and powerfully.

I made various pacts with my mentors over the years, which require me to share my magickal knowledge. I am a member of The Gallery of Magick. There are seventeen of us, and we have been working for over three decades to develop practical magick. I am pleased to begin sharing our work with this book, and I have made a commitment to only share magick that works well.

Too much money magick is weak or unworkable, and that's a shame because it makes people believe that magick doesn't work, or that money magick is somehow unspiritual. I want to change that by putting powerful, practical magick in your hands.

When used well, money magick is a relatively easy way to bring more money into your life.

I'm confident that the methods in this book are powerful enough that you'll get what you came looking for, and more besides. Just make sure you read the whole book, and understand everything before you begin.

But can this really work? Isn't it just a money-making scam? I've worked as an author (under another name) for a few decades, and I can assure you that these days writing books is not the best way to get rich, so that's not why I share these secrets. The magick is genuine. It brings real results. It's shared now so that you can see the reality of magick, which can lead you on many wonderful journeys. With magick, you can live your dreams the way you want to live them.

Does it work for everybody? If you look at the reviews, you'll see that some people say, 'It does not work.' But there's always a reason. The magick *does* work. It works for *most* people. You can see that in most of the reviews, as well as in thousands of posts on our website. People really do find success.

So why doesn't it work for everybody? Some people expect instant cash and lottery wins. Some don't read the instructions. Some don't settle into the work, and many are impatient. You need to read the book carefully, you need to be patient, you need to let the results come when they come, and you need to avoid desperation. If you are able to do that, the magick *will* work. And when it does, that's a beautiful feeling.

Ancient and New

Why is this book a mix of ancient secrets and new technology? If you've done a lot of magick before, you'll know that there are millions upon millions of opinions and theories about magick. People stay up late arguing about what works, why it works and how to make it work.

Some say that ancient secrets are worthless. Some say you don't need any magickal tools so long as you have imagination. Others suggest that you need to perform every gesture and ritual exactly the way it was written in an ancient grimoire, or you will never get results.

Thankfully, whatever the exact truth about magick may be, *magick works*. I've found that it works by using new ideas and ancient secrets.

Rather than trying to decide which theory is best, or why magick works, I'll simply provide you with the fastest and most practical money magick that can solve a lot of your financial problems.

The magick in this book is based around the creation of a Magickal Cashbook, which is a way of connecting several forms of magick with your clear intention to make more money.

The Cashbook is nothing more than a small, simple notebook, painted with colors and symbols. You charge the book using a fairly basic magick ritual and then write in the amount of money you want to attract. The money then manifests, often in an unexpected way. It takes only days to work.

I've described this in a mundane way, but the book is far from mundane. When it works for you, you will realize that you have created an object of genuine power.

You may wonder why magick works. It doesn't matter why magick works, but I know that many people worry about this, even though the time taken to perform such simple magick is minimal. This curiosity is fine, but the best way to learn about magick is to use magick, and the more you use it, the more you understand how it works.

When magick begins to work, you may *really* begin to wonder why it works, and you may find, as many do, that when you attract a large sum of money, you feel guilty. Do you have the right to take this money from the world? This guilty feeling usually passes.

But when you see that the world responds to your magick, you will begin to wonder about your place in the universe and the meaning of magick. This is a good thing, and a pleasant side-effect, but it should not be your aim. Your aim should be to get magick working.

Many would disagree and say that the only purpose of magick is to contact your Holy Guardian Angel and heal others. In my experience, there's no substitute for *doing magick and getting results*. The better you are at practical magick, the better you will be at *any* spiritual work.

For every magician who actually does magick, there are countless who simply think or read about magick. If you only think about magick, nothing magickal will ever happen. Practice the magick in this book, and you will see things change.

There are three key requirements for successful magick, and they are easy to achieve. I will not force you to find rare herbs, create complex tools or meditate for hours. This book is about taking the shortest possible route to magickal success. The key requirements are:

A clear intent.

A precise magickal method.

A certain state of mind.

I'll show you exactly how to get all three right.

I can't tell you why magick works, whether the spirits are real or imaginary, whether we're using quantum physics or mere imagination. I have theories and beliefs, but I won't bore you with them. Instead, I will put the magick in your hands and let you come up with your own ideas about why it works.

The methods in this book will cost you almost nothing, in terms of time or money, but will bring you great rewards. You don't even have to believe. You can act out the rituals, and so long as you do it with the conviction that an actor would, *as though it is real*, then your belief doesn't matter at all. The magick will work.

The magick in my books has been developed by The Gallery of Magick to get results safely. There is plenty of evil in the world, but there is no evil in this book. You will not be punished by karma or chased down by demons. Magick is about taking control of your life, rather than being controlled by circumstances, people or random chaos. Taking control of your life with magick is your divine right.

You may also worry about payback, and whether there are dangers. You can trust me when I say that this magick is very safe, and there is never any backlash. Some people worry that magick gives an unfair advantage, and so that means the universe will find a way of taking the money back from you. None of this is true. It's pure superstition, and it ignores a very obvious fact: the universe is not in balance, and it is not fair, especially when it comes to money. There is an unbelievable lack of equality in the world. People live in luxury with billions in the bank, and the universe never punishes them or balances it out. Other people live in poverty and the universe never balances it out. So, put the idea of universal balance out of your mind. It doesn't exist, and it's your right to attract more money than you have now.

Others hear stories that magick will cause a horrible accident, to bring the money to you through an insurance claim or inheritance. Again, this is disinformation designed to scare you away from magick. In all the decades that I have worked with magick, I have never seen such disasters occur. It's actually quite easy to get money flowing, and magick won't cause havoc, because it doesn't need to.

Magick gives you the *choice* to increase your level of income, and there is no universal force that will take it away from you. You need to feel comfortable with money, and avoid feeling guilty about money magick. Make sure you're relaxed about having more than you have now. If you resent other people making money, or feel that money is evil or the cause of all the world's ills, it will be much harder for you to welcome money. The more you can see money as an opportunity for pleasure, sharing, satisfaction and freedom, the easier it will come to you.

I have been using magick since I was twelve years old, and I've used just about every system and idea you can imagine. A lot of magick worked. A lot didn't. Some magick felt amazingly real and powerful but brought no tangible results. Other kinds of magick felt like they couldn't possibly have worked, but brought great results.

The work presented in this book contains my insights into the magick that worked best for me when I was still young. I know it has worked for others. It can work for you too. It continues to work for me today.

We've taken the simplest and most powerful systems, and streamlined them into a series of steps that get money magick working for you as fast as possible.

The Magickal Cashbook works with a spirit called Nitika, who can bring wealth. As many people have found, Nitika is an amazing spirit, easy to contact, who brings cash fast.

Nitika is neither an angel or demon, but is thought of as a genius spirit or 'personified virtue.' We think of Nitika as a combination of angelic powers expressed through a single spirit. Nitika is a very gentle yet powerful spirit and is listed as one of The Genii of the Twelve Hours in the *Nuctemeron*, attributed to Apollonius of Tyana from the First Century AD. Nitika was made known to English readers through a translation of Éliphas Lévi's 1897 book of *Transcendental Magic*. The magick of Nitika has been around for a long time but remains relevant and workable today.

Many spirits can be conjured if you know their name and sigil. Some spirits will help if you simply say their name in the right circumstances. There is no doubt that Nitika can be conjured through a direct call, and through the help of other magickal operations, but nothing gives you faster contact with this spirit than the right sigil.

A sigil, or seal, as it is sometimes known, is a drawing that gives you direct access to a spirit. This book contains the only known copy of Nitika's seal. This sigil cannot be found in any other author's book. It is like a secret key to powerful magick.

Using this sigil, and the streamlined methods I give you, there's almost nothing to stop bursts of money coming into your life.

How Much Money Can You Make?

It's important to remember where you're starting from. If you're in poverty, I will not promise that you'll be a millionaire. I will not promise lottery wins. I will not claim that you can attract undreamt-of riches. To do so would be to lie, and I don't want to trick you. So, I will tell you the truth.

I spent some time in magick forums back in 2009, reading discussions of magickal results, and I was astonished to see people getting excited about attracting an extra $100. Some were even glad to get just $20 through magick. This surprised me.

To me, $100 is a small amount of money. On a good day, I could earn that in a few minutes, so why spend half an hour doing a ritual to attract such a tiny sum?

But then I remembered that when I was poor, in my early twenties, I would have been just as impressed by $100. The money I make, even today, would not impress somebody much wealthier than me.

$20,000 might be impressive to some people, but to a multi-millionaire, that amount would not seem quite so impressive. To a billionaire, it would seem trivial. This is why it's important to compare your magickal result to what you had before.

The point of this is to make sure that you recognize the gains you make. If you are extremely poor, magick can make you much wealthier, much faster than you expect. If you are rich, it can make money you never dreamed possible. But each person has their own starting point. *Magick builds on your starting point.*

If $100 is what you really need, you won't become a millionaire this year. But if you already deal in millions, then magick can push you to earn hundreds of millions. Please don't fool yourself though – if you are on a low income, you are highly unlikely to earn great wealth quickly.

The great news is that if you're starting from a low income, you can use magick to build your wealth steadily. Each time you use magick, you can take a financial leap. And the first steps you take will bring a surprising amount of money. We have seen this happen to so many people who have used this book.

Getting to a place that you now think of as 'rich' will take time, but it will take less time than you can imagine. One thing is certain, if you *don't* use magick, you are highly unlikely to break out of your current financial state.

We love stories about people who rise from rags to riches, and it's true that people can use talent, skill and hard work to make that leap. But for most people, the most likely thing is that - no matter how hard you work - you stay in the same financial zone. Magick can push you out of that zone.

Your First Big Break

Decide now, what amount will be impressive, unexpected and exciting to you. If $20 would excite you, be honest, and say you want $20. If you'd be amazed by $1000, that's also fine. If you're already wealthy, and wouldn't be impressed unless you make $100,000 of extra income out of the blue, then you need to be certain of that too.

The reason for this is that money *will* turn up when you make your Magical Cashbook. When it does, I want you to know that the magick worked.

Sometimes, you might find a monthly expense is $50 less than expected. That's a result. Sometimes you might find $20 stuffed down the side of a chair. That's a result. Or you might get a promotion or a bonus. And there are hundreds, if not thousands, of creative ways that magick can provide the money. Don't expect the money to come in a particular way. Let it come in any way, at any speed, and then it will come fast and creatively.

It would be sad if you dismissed the magick, and said, 'Oh, that's just a coincidence.' In reality, it is usually a series of chance events and encounters that lead to magickal success. So when you see coincidence, welcome it and know that the magick helped. The more grateful you feel for your results, the more likely you are to get them in the future.

Decide now what amount would convince you that magick is real, and then write it down somewhere secret. If this amount turns up, you know you can trust this book to help you, and you can keep using magick.

Magick usually makes you a little bit more money than you think is possible. You need to consider that statement carefully.

If you'd be excited by $100, then you'll probably make slightly more than that on your first attempt at making money with magick. And if you need $50,000, then that's what you'll get, and perhaps a little bit more. If $50 would be a true thrill, you should make more than $50.

But if you're the sort of person who's in true poverty, and if $100 is a big deal to you, I will not lie and say you can win the lottery or make $50,000 out of nowhere. You can get there eventually. You can get there faster than you thought possible. But expect your *own personal surprise* and an amount of money that is meaningful to *you*.

One problem with most money magick is that it takes time to work. The Magickal Cashbook works fast. You can get some money quickly, almost instantly. Then you can use the rituals to attract steady income and bursts of money. But it's really important that you don't *insist* that it works fast. You need to let the results come when they come, in whatever way they come. I've often said if you can wait a year for something, magick makes it happen instantly, but if you insist it happens instantly, you might have to wait a year.

You can work on this, by learning patience. The more patient you are, the faster you get what you want. If you don't get what you want the first time, keep going, knowing that magick *is* real. That sort of trust and involvement with magick is so much more powerful than doing one ritual and hoping for a big result. Magick is not about hope, but about shaping your reality.

If you want to win the lottery, that's quite normal, most people do. But if you're serious about making more money, I'd advise you to give up the lottery altogether. When you give up random gambling, you're sending a message out to the universe that you trust that money will turn up. That is way more powerful than hoping for a win.

Also, I have to be upfront and say that most people find magick doesn't work for lotteries. Magick is only one way of influencing the world, and when you enter a lottery, you are up against the powers of random effects and astronomical odds. Even the strongest ritual will struggle to change the way those numbers fall.

A more successful approach is to use magick to guess the correct numbers in advance. That way, you're not trying to influence the fall of numbers itself - you're merely trying to use magick to select the right numbers for yourself. But magick is more fun than a lottery win. When you see money conjure its way into your life on a regular basis, you don't need a lottery win. When you feel comfortable with that, the magick will work even faster.

Since this book was first published in 2014, there's one story that I've been told over and over again. Somebody does their first ritual and asks for $5000 or $1000 or something that is way out of reach for them. Nothing happens. They give up. But then a few months later they try again, and they try for something that is just out of reach, and it works – maybe $20 maybe $200 - and then all the rituals begin to work. Consider this carefully, and avoid desperation and demanding too much. Seek what would be exciting for you, but not an absurd amount. If you build steadily, you get to a place of riches much faster than if you demand riches right now.

It's true that there are stories online and in reviews where people have made thousands in a few days, with the Magickal Cashbook, and others even more, but don't let the big success stories put you off from starting small. You may get a pleasant surprise, and more than you hoped for, but be willing to build gradually. The big amounts come to those with natural magickal abilities and a high level of patience. It can take time to build those skills, so go in with an open mind.

Although your mind should be open, try to avoid testing the magick. If you perform it as an experiment to see if it will work and then stare at your watch waiting for a result, I know it will *not* work. Perform it as though it is real, and assume it will work.

Follow Instructions, Experiment Later

In time, you will learn enough about magick that you will want to adapt these methods. That is good because nothing is more powerful than your own, personal magick. But to begin with, follow the instructions as set out and you will get the best results.

Also, try to be quite casual about the instructions. That is, follow them closely, but don't worry too much about getting things perfectly correct. If you mess up a little, it still tends to work.

I am constantly astonished by endless discussions about how to pronounce Words of Power, how to enact a certain ritual, and so on. People worry about magick, rather than getting on with it. If you do the magick as instructed, with clear intent, it will create the correct state of mind, and then results will follow.

When you go to start your car in the morning, you don't hope and pray that it will start. You don't need faith or belief. You just expect that your car will start and it usually does. The same approach works with magick.

You may wonder if you really need to make the Cashbook. Yes, you do. I know that many people don't want to make the Cashbook, because who wants a strange little magick book lying around their house, covered in magickal sigils? Wouldn't it be easier just to chant a spell?

When you make something in the real world, the magick is often more likely to manifest in the real world. You are creating something in the physical world and charging it with magickal power. That has a strong effect.

The magickal book is easy to make and easy to hide, and it's best to keep it away from prying eyes.

There are many articles on The Gallery of Magick website to help you get the magick working if you encounter any problems at all. The main message is to be relaxed and casual about your magick. But it is worth reading everything that's on there. We've put the equivalent of three books worth of information on the website, and it's all free. You can learn a lot about magick.

Making Room for Results

Read any book on magick, and you will find one theme that comes up over and over again; *lust for result*. It is said that if you lust desperately for results, then you will not get them. But this is a strange irony because if you go to the trouble of performing magick, it must be because you *want* the results. So how do you let go of this lust?

Many people perform their magick and then try their best to forget the result they want. While it is true that this 'letting go' will bring results fast, it is not easy to achieve. And when the magickal result is important to you, forgetting the result is almost impossible to achieve.

Here's what often happens. Somebody performs a spell or ritual. Let's say the result they want is to sell their novel to a particular publisher. They send off the novel, and as the weeks go by, they can't stop thinking about selling their novel. So, every day they check their email, fantasize about signing books at a bookshop, or feel startled when the phone rings, hoping it just might be the publisher. This is a classic case of lusting after the result, and it not only short-circuits the magick, but it can cause the magick to work in reverse. You're pestering the magick instead of giving it the freedom to work.

Sadly, many people deal with their lust for result with a form of panic. Let's take the above example. Our writer sends the novel off to the publisher. A few days later, the thought occurs that it would be great to sell that novel. In a panic, knowing that lust for result might ruin the working, our writer tries not to think about the novel or the magick. For the following weeks, huge amounts of mental energy are exerted on *pretending* there is no desire.

You're not fooling anybody when this happens. Your desire is real. And lust can, in fact, be a powerful force for manifestation, but that is a subject for another book. For now, you need to deal with your desires practically to prevent a magickal short circuit.

Lust for result is a challenge, but there is no need to pretend you have no desire. Here is a way to beat your *lust for result*. Every time you remember your magick or the result you want, feel glad that you remembered, and imagine how good it will feel when the magickal result comes to pass. Imagine that the result has *already* happened and that you feel *relief*. That's all there is to it.

Read that paragraph again and again if you need to. When your desire comes into your mind, let yourself feel relief, as though you already have what you want. That defuses the lust. Your desire is still there, it's still real and strong, but this is the opposite of hoping or wishing. It takes some mental energy, but rather than trying to suppress or hide thoughts and feelings, you modify them slightly.

If you have trouble feeling good about your desire, here's a powerful trick. Think of a memory or image that makes you feel good, happy or grateful. It doesn't matter what you use but think of something that creates a potent emotion. The moment you remember your magick or the magickal result you are seeking, conjure up this memory, feel the positive emotion, and then continue to think about your result.

Don't avoid your result. Feel free to think about it. Feel good that the result has come to pass. Even though a part of you knows the result hasn't occurred yet, imagine that it *has* occurred, and imagine what it feels like to have the result and to be grateful for it.

If you find yourself wondering about *how* it will work, or *why* it will work, or *when* it will work – that is lust for result. If that happens, then you need to busy yourself to stop this rush of thoughts. Pondering on magickal results is a form of doubt, and is best avoided. The more patient you are, the faster results will come.

But don't worry about *lust for result*. Feel free to think about the result you want, but think about it with a warm glow.

Never waste your time worrying about when results will come, how fast they will come, or in what form they will arrive.

This last point is a very important one. Sometimes magick requires us to be specific. If you want to stop an enemy, you bind that specific person. That can be more powerful than if you put out a general protection spell. So being specific can be hugely powerful. In more general magick, though, it can be a mistake to be too specific. If you perform a spell to make money by getting a raise, and that's the *only* way you want the money to come, you are cutting yourself off from other opportunities.

The universe, or the spirits, can probably think of a thousand better ways to get money to you, so let it come in *whatever form it wants*.

Be open to new avenues of income, and the income will flow.

Making Your Magickal Cashbook

Buy a notebook. It's that easy. You could spend hours making your own notebook out of fresh parchment, gluing it together with traditional binding methods, but it's far quicker to buy a notebook. It will work well.

If you can buy something that looks or feels vaguely magickal to you, so much the better, but it isn't vital. Ideally, there should be no lines on the paper, but again, it is not vital.

You should paint the front cover gray or silver, and paint the back cover orange. You can stick on card or paper if it's easier. You can do this using cheap paints and a basic brush. You can get what you need at an art shop or just look for something cheap around town. Nothing fancy is required. These colors act almost like a battery, drawing magickal energy through the book when you perform the ritual.

The only problem you will face is that it may take several coats of paint to cover up the writing and logos on the cover. If that's what it takes, then keep going until all you have are clear gray and orange covers.

A shortcut is to glue white paper or card onto the cover of your notebook, and then paint that, or use colored card or paper. It doesn't have to be too special. The inside of the cover does not need to be colored.

You may have a thousand questions about the notebook - what size, what style of binding, what weight and so on. Really, you don't need to worry. So long as you have a notebook of some kind, with pages to write on, and a gray cover, with an orange back cover, the magick will work.

On the front cover, you will need a copy of the following sigil. It can be drawn by hand, photocopied or printed out from the website.

For most people, drawing is out of the question, so it's completely OK to photocopy it from the book. If you're using the e-book, then you can download the image and print it out, or even photograph the e-book and print that out.

You can find the image here:

http://galleryofmagick.com/images/

You can stick the printout on the front of your Cashbook, and that will do fine. You might want to trace over the printed image, lightly, with a pen or pencil, to connect yourself to the sigil. It might look something like this:

If you have the confidence, you can draw this as it's shown above. Use pen, pencil, or any kind of ink. As a rule, it's best to use black ink or dark pencil.

Copying the Hebrew words might take some practice if you're not used to writing in Hebrew. Practice on blank paper first. But even if you make a bit of a mess, it doesn't matter, because you will soon perform a brief ritual that dedicates the book to Nitika.

If you cannot copy exactly, don't worry. If you get the basic shapes of the letters right, it will work. And if you prefer to print out or photocopy, that is also fine, but it does help if you then take the time to draw lightly over the image with a pencil or pen, to connect yourself to the shapes and images. You do not need to be able to understand the various divine names and words of power, so long as you can see them.

On the orange back cover draw or glue a copy of this sigil:

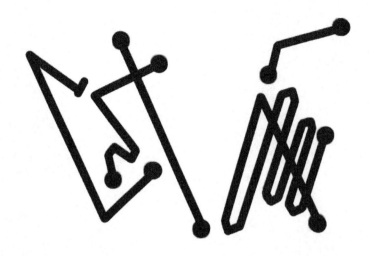

This should again be drawn using black ink, pencil or pen, or feel free to use a printout. Once again, if you use a photocopy or printout, take the time to trace over the lines lightly with a pen or pencil.

Open your book and on the first blank page of the book write the following words of power:

NAH-KAH EE-AH-OH-EH

These words of power are a statement that means it is your will to recognize God, and this gives you the authority to work the magick.

Once you have written that down, say the words out loud. The AH sound appears in a lot of these words, and this AH is like the *a* in *father*. The words are pronounced as follows.

NAH sounds like *ah* with *n* at the front.

KAH sounds like *ah* with *k* at the front.

EE sounds like *me* without the *m*.

AH is the word *ah*.

OH is the word *oh*.

EH sounds like *yeah* without the *y*.

Accurate pronunciation is not important, but I know people worry about it, so I'm making it as clear as possible. Remember that a bold and confident attitude is far more important than correct pronunciation. If you need more details, you can find them on the *Pronunciation and Spelling FAQ* page at **www.galleryofmagick.com** where there's a video showing you exactly how to say the words.

You've now built your Magickal Cashbook, and all you need to do is empower it. Then you can begin to write your petitions in the book to manifest money.

Empowering your Cashbook

In the following empowering ritual, you will use the name Nitika. There are two main ways to pronounce this, so use the one that feels easiest to you.

One way is to say KNEE-TEA-CAR, where you are literally using the English words **knee**, **tea**, and **car**.

A second pronunciation is KNEE-TEA-CAH. Again, you use **knee** and **tea**. CAH sounds like **calm** without the **lm**. (You can think of CAH as a sound that rhymes with **ma** or **pa**. So CAH is just like **ma** but with a **c** instead of an **m**.)

For the rest of this book, I will use KNEE-TEA-CAH, but you can substitute it with the other pronunciation if you prefer. It will work.

You should also learn to vibrate the name, which is just a fancy occult term for letting the word really rumble out of you. When you speak, let the name come up from your belly, through the back of your throat. Make it feel as though you are giving birth to the word as you speak, rather than just whispering it.

If this sounds puzzling, imagine how an actor would say a magickal name in a horror movie – they would let it rumble from deep within, almost gurgling through their throat in a deep roar. Weirdly enough, Hollywood has it right, and it helps to be this dramatic.

Whatever type of voice you have, try to let the name of Nitika rumble through your throat. By vibrating the name in this way, it has much more power. The same is true of all magickal Words of Power used in this book. The rest of the ritual can be spoken normally, but *all* the words in capitals should be vibrated as above.

If you need to work in private, you can whisper the words, or even say them in your head, but if you do, you must *imagine* them rumbling out of you loudly, to the very ends of the universe.

When you feel ready, find a time to be alone and calm your thoughts. Have a pen ready.

Do not think about your needs or money. Instead, spend some time thinking about something that you enjoy or like. Just ponder that for a while, breathing easily. Then, without giving much thought to what you're doing, perform the following steps.

1. Open your Cashbook and vibrate the words: NAH-KAH EE-AH-OH-EH.

2. Close the Cashbook and stare at the center of the sigil on its front cover. Do not stare hard, but let your gaze move over the sigil and consider that this is a key that unlocks access to the spirit Nitika.

3. Still looking at the sigil, vibrate the name Nitika (KNEE-TEA-CAH) eleven times. Count on your fingers if you have to. Make sure that minimal effort goes into counting, and most of your effort goes into feeling the name in your throat and drinking in the sigil with your eyes. Know that you are actually calling to Nitika and that Nitika will now be aware of you.

4. Open the book. Just below the words NAH-KAH EE-AH-OH-EH, write the following words:

'Nitika. Nitika. Nitika. In the name of EH-HE-YEAH, EE-AH-OH-EH ELL-OH-HEEM, and EE-AH-OH-EH ELL-OH-AH-VAH-DAH-ART I call on Nitika, Nitika, Nitika. Oh Spirit Nitika, I command thee to shape the past and the future to bring me wealth.'

[Here leave a space and draw a small circle, about the size of an average coin]

Now write:

34

'I command thee to bring me wealth in the names of SHAD-EYE-ELK-EYE and ADD-OH-NIGH-HA-AH-RETZ. Go now, and be ready to come when I call you. Go in peace, and cause no harm to me or my loved ones. Go!'

You do not need to say these words out loud yet.

The words you have written might look something like this:

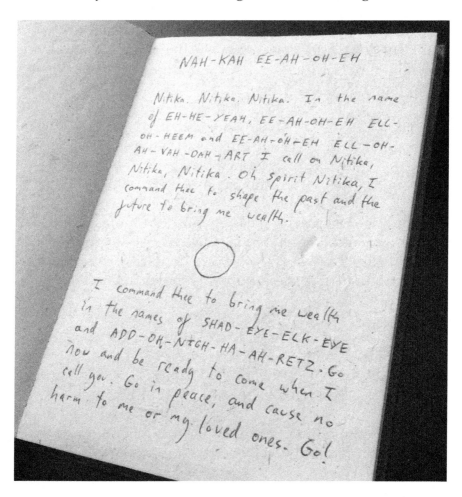

5. When you've finished writing, close the book and turn it face down, so that you can see the orange side and the symbol that resides there. Leave the book for a few minutes, and then put it away for at least an hour. Just put it out of sight and get on with your day.

Your Magickal Cashbook is now ready to attract money. When you actually use the Cashbook, you will need to read the Words of Power out loud. These are traditional Hebrew words, rendered in a form that is easy for English speakers to work with. The Words of Power used in the ritual are all Divine names. The words are:

Ehyeh
Iao-eh Elohim
Iao-eh Eloah Va-Daath
Shaddai El Chai
Adonai ha-Aretz

These words have been used in magick for many centuries. They are an encoding of divine authority. Although they may look difficult to say at first, they are quite easy to pronounce. The pronunciation of these words, as shown in the ritual is:

EH-HE-YEAH
EE-AH-OH-EH ELL-OH-HEEM
EE-AH-OH-EH ELL-OH-AH-VAH-DAH-ART
SHAD-EYE-ELK-EYE
ADD-OH-NIGH-HA-AH-RETZ

The pronunciation is simple, but in case you need more guidance, this is a detailed look at each word of power.

EH-HE-YEAH
EH is the same as *yeah* without the y.
HE is the word *he*.
YEAH is just like the word *yeah*.

36

EE-AH-OH-EH ELL-OH-HEEM

EE sounds like *me* without the *m*.

AH is the word *ah*.

OH is the word *oh*.

EH sounds like *yeah* without the *y*.

ELL is the same as *bell* without a *b*.

OH is the word *oh*.

HEEM is the same as *deem*, but with *h* instead of *d*.

EE-AH-OH-EH ELL-OH-AH-VAH-DAH-ART

EE sounds like *me* without the *m*.

AH is the word *ah*.

OH is the word *oh*.

EH sounds like *yeah* without the *y*.

ELL is the same as *bell* without a *b*.

OH is the word *oh*.

AH is the word *ah*.

VAH is like *ah* with *v* at the front.

DAH is like *dark* without the *k*.

ART is the word *art*.

SHAD-EYE-ELK-EYE

SHAD is like *bad* but with *sh* instead of *b*.

EYE is like *eye*.

ELK is like *elk*.

EYE is like *eye*.

ADD-OH-NIGH-HA-AH-RETZ

ADD is the word *add*.

OH is the word *oh*.

NIGH is the same *night* without the *t*.

HA is the same as the word *harp* without *rp*.

AH is the word *ah*.

RETZ is like *rats* but with an *e* instead of an *a*.

With these words learned, you are ready to go.

Using Your Cashbook to Attract Money

Now that your Cashbook has been empowered, you need to learn the basic ritual for using it. Here's exactly what you do during the Attraction Ritual.

1. Perform this Attraction Ritual once a day, at any time of day. If you miss a day, it's not the end of the world, but aim for eleven consecutive days. This shows commitment. If *you* demonstrate commitment, so will Nitika. If you don't find the time, why should Nitika bother? If the money turns up before the eleven days are over, you can end the ritual, of course.

2. Sit in a quiet place where you won't be disturbed. Open your book and vibrate the words NAH-KAH EE-AH-OH-EH over and over until you feel a sense of calm come over you. If you feel nothing, don't worry, just stay relaxed and move onto the next step.

3. Close the book and gaze at the sigil of Nitika on the cover. Think of the amount of money you want to create. Most importantly, think about what you'll *do* with this money. (See the next chapter for precise details on this point.) When you've got the feeling of the money you want to attract, vibrate the name Nitika *three* times while looking at the sigil.

4. Open the book and vibrate NAH-KAH EE-AH-OH-EH one more time, and then read out the first part of the invocation, starting with, 'Nitika. Nitika. Nitika. In the name...' using the pronunciations that you have learned.

When you get to the small circle that you drew, stop.

5. Turn to the *next blank page* in your book and write the amount you want to attract. In this example, it is $50, but you should choose an amount that's right for you. Write $50 and put a circle

around it. Use this same page each day, adding another circle each time you perform the ritual. (If you use a different currency, write down that currency.) After three days, it would look something like this:

6. Now turn back to the first page and read everything that follows the small circle, starting with, 'I command thee...'

7. When you have finished reading, close the book, put it away and do something else.

8. Remember what was said about *lust for result*. It's almost impossible to stop thinking about your ritual, but it helps if you do something involving, such as making and eating food, going out, singing, calling somebody, or anything that involves physical exercise. If you find yourself dwelling on the ritual, remember to feel grateful for the result.

That's it. Repeat each day. It might take a day or two for results to show up. It might take eleven days. It might take longer, but the money will turn up. It may turn up in a highly unexpected way. The more patient and relaxed you are, the more likely it is that the money will come.

Don't wait for it or look for it, but be glad when it does arrive. *If it doesn't arrive when you want it to, don't write the ritual off as a failure.* Know that it may yet manifest. When the eleven days are over, you can start a new ritual for a different amount.

When you do see the money turn up, know that the magick has worked (even if it's not the exact amount you asked for). Go back to your Cashbook, turn to the page where you wrote the amount of money you were seeking, and draw a cross through each circle where you wrote the amount. As you do so, feel gratitude. When you feel gratitude, you are paying the spirit back with your emotions, and that makes for good future relations.

If nothing seems to have happened after eleven days, cross everything out on the money page, feeling grateful for your result (*as though it really has happened*) and start a fresh page as soon as you're ready. Starting a new ritual can help you to forget about the previous one, which opens the doorway to success.

What to Think and Feel During the Ritual

When you're performing the ritual, and get to Step 3, it's important to think about what you'll *do* with the money. Be honest. It's absolutely vital that you don't try to be worthy or spiritual or generous in an attempt to impress Nitika.

If you want $1000 to pay for a new sound system, then that's what you want. Don't lie to yourself and Nitika by thinking that you could give the money to charity or share it with friends. Giving is powerful, and I'll cover it in another book, but it is not a part of what you're doing here.

What you are doing is putting your emotion into the ritual. You're not trying to appear like a good person. The spirits don't care. Nitika doesn't care what you're going to do with the money, so long as your desire for extra money is *sincere*. So if you can pass on that feeling of sincerity during the ritual, Nitika is more likely to respond.

Asking a spirit to help is one thing, but showing *why* you are asking is quite another. So, when it gets to Step 3, think about how good it will feel to get the money, and what you'll spend it on.

Don't worry about how the money will turn up. This is vital. Just think about having the money and spending it in the way you want. Enjoy the sensation as though it's happening now. It's the same feeling you get when a relative unexpectedly hands you a wad of cash, or when you win an unexpected prize. Get that *feeling*, just for a moment, and move on.

Don't stress about this stage. All you're doing is thinking about what you plan to do with the money. But be aware that you are making a pact with Nitika. If you ask for money for a sound system – when unexpected money turns up, spend it on that. Nitika will then respond more powerfully next time you ask for help. It's important to keep your side of the bargain, unless circumstances make it impossible.

When you speak to Nitika and use words such as 'I command thee' you should speak with authority, but not as somebody trying to overpower the spirit. Think of the way a good manager would talk to employees. You don't beg your workers to help, and you don't plead with them. But nor do you order them about like an army commander.

When it comes to magick, you are neither a beggar or an army officer. Think of yourself as a manager. The spirits are there to work for you. All you need to do is tell them what you want, politely, with a tone of firm authority, and you will get what you want.

But, most importantly, a good manager is openly grateful to employees. And the best managers show gratitude before the job is even done. Imagine a good boss saying, 'Can you clear those back-orders for me by lunchtime? Thanks so much.'

When you have a manager like that – and it's rare – you are far more likely to get the job done. If the boss begs or pleads, or worse, orders you about, you don't work as well. Spirits are like workers, and they will work for you, but don't treat them like slaves. Just because they are there to work for you doesn't mean you should disrespect them.

Your gratitude can be genuine and heartfelt but doesn't need to be fawning. Your gratitude is the same as a wage. It's what a spirit expects as payment, so keep that feeling in mind when performing the ritual.

Magick Works

Magick works, but it doesn't always work the way you expect. I once performed an elaborate ritual to find a low-cost house, and as soon as it was done a relative offered to sell me a house with $100,000 knocked off the price. Not what I expected, but a result, and a good result at that. So be aware of money turning up in unexpected ways.

But what if it doesn't work? You may have asked for too much or too little, or you may just need more practice.

A good trick to get the magick working is this: use the Cashbook to attract something really small, but incredibly specific. So, if you need $500, just forget that for now. Instead, try requesting an obscure amount such as 50c or $3. Something that feels so easy it's almost pointless to do magick for.

This works, because it's such a small amount, and then your disbelief falls away. You let go of all lust for result, because who cares about 50c anyway? But when this specific amount turns up out of the blue, within a few days, it lets you know that magick works. Even though it's for a tiny amount, it gives you more trust in the magick. It's an easy and fun way to get things started but think of it as an enjoyable way to do magick, rather than that you are testing the magick. The moment you test magick, you're lacking trust, and that can short-circuit everything. (Remember also that the Cashbook often throws in a little extra on top of what you request. So, if you ask for a very specific $3, don't be surprised if you get $3.30.)

The Cashbook works well for most people if the instructions are followed closely, but if you're having trouble getting started, give this a try and it should get things flowing. Money finds a way.

If you want huge changes in your financial circumstances, where your focus is on building a career that generates extreme wealth, look into my book *Magickal Riches*. That is a much more involved text, but it works if you want to take wealth magick to the next level.

The magick in this book works easily for most people, but if you find it difficult, The Gallery of Magick website and blog contains many FAQs, along with advice and practical information that is updated on a regular basis.

www.galleryofmagick.com

The Gallery of Magick Facebook page will also keep you up to date.

If you have an interest in developing your magick further, there are many texts that can assist you.

Words of Power and *The Greater Words of Power* present an extremely simple ritual practice, for bringing about change in yourself and others, as well as directing and attracting changed circumstances.

Magickal Protection contains rituals that can be directed at specific problems, as well as a daily practice called The Sword Banishing, which is one of our most popular and effective rituals.

For those who cannot find peace through protection, there is *Magickal Attack*, by Gordon Winterfield. Gordon has also written Demons of Magick, a comprehensive guide to working safely with demonic power. Dark magick is not to everybody's taste, but this is a highly moral approach that puts the emphasis on using personal sincerity.

For those seeking more money, *Magickal Riches* is comprehensive, with rituals for everything from gambling to sales, with a master ritual to oversee magickal income. For the more ambitious, *Wealth Magick* contains a complex set of rituals for earning money by building a career. For those still trying to find their feet, there is *The Magickal Job Seeker*.

The 72 Sigils of Power, by Zanna Blaise, covers Contemplation Magic (for insight and wisdom) and Results Magic (for changing the world around you). Zanna is also the author of *The Angels of Love*, which uses a tasking method with six angels to heal relationships or to attract a soulmate.

Magickal Seduction is a text that looks at attracting others by using magick to amplify your attractive qualities, rather than through deception. *Adventures in Sex Magick* is a more specialized text, for those open-minded enough to explore this somewhat extreme form of magick.

The Master Works of Chaos Magick by Adam Blackthorne is an overview of self-directed and creative magick, which also includes a section covering the Olympic Spirits. *Magickal Servitors* takes another aspect of Chaos Magick and updates it into a modern, workable method.

The 72 Angels of Magick is our most comprehensive book of angel magick and explores hundreds of powers that can be applied by working with these angels. *The Angels of Alchemy* works with 42 angels, to obtain personal transformation.

Our most successful book is *Sigils of Power and Transformation* by Adam Blackthorne, which has brought great results to many people. *Archangels of Magick* by Damon Brand is the most complete book of magick we have published, covering sigils, divination, invocation, and evocation.

Damon Brand

www.galleryofmagick.com

Printed in Great Britain
by Amazon

27935904R00030